I0756336

FINISHING LINE PRESS
www.finishinglinepress.com

The Unfolding

poems by

Nancy Sobanik

Finishing Line Press
Georgetown, Kentucky

The Unfolding

ISBN 979-8-89990-480-6 First Edition

ACKNOWLEDGMENTS

Grateful acknowledgment is made to the editors of the following journals in which some of these poems (or earlier versions of them) originally appeared:

One Art, "The Unfolding of the Calyx"
Triggerfish Critical Review, "Bindings"
Anti-Heroin Chic, "Room of Mirrors"
Sheila-Na-Gig, "Flying Kites at the Cape"
Sparks of Calliope, "Morning Swim;" "Pilgrimage" (Best of the Net Nomination 2023 and Pushcart Prize Nomination 2024)
Verse- Virtual, "Sun Glint"
Frost Meadow Review, "Morning"
Verse-Virtual, "Great Blue Heron at Robert's Pond"

Publisher: Leah Huete de Maines
Editor: Christen Kincaid
Cover Art: Justin Cory
Author Photo: Nancy Sobanik
Cover Design: Elizabeth Maines McCleavy

Order online: www.finishinglinepress.com
also available on amazon.com

Author inquiries and mail orders:
Finishing Line Press
PO Box 1626
Georgetown, Kentucky 40324
USA

Contents

The Unfolding of the Calyx

The buds have come,
first beech then aspen,
and catkin litter falls everywhere.
I pull it from the cowl of the windshield,
wipe pollen off the glass,
the back of my sleeve yellow.

They'll suddenly be gone in a week
as crabgrass blades its way
through last year's leaf mold,
parting it like the Red Sea.
My own twisted sepals
are just beginning to unwind.

For four years a hurricane
of death flung my severed heart
onto stone-strewn ground,
trampled hollowed chambers
into a juiceless plum.

I contemplate the trees—
do they feel relief at the end
of battering by winter winds?
Do they hum a song only they hear
when sap awakens to flow
like ice out on the river?

Trees will snap leaves open
into green whispering fans.
I gather pale lemon daffodils
into a blue glass vase.
My fist that holds the flower
will unfold, palm open and up,
offering and receiving.
The blush of blood once more
will petal my cheeks.

Bindings

I slid into time, that primordial broth,
skin scrunched, soon swaddled
in snug cloth used to soothe
and regulate a fretful neonate.

My father carried in his gut a mountain
of rope, a coiled halyard twisted into knots.
His fingers bled raw,
but his sail was never raised.

He spun new ropes of words
from the pith of uneaten fruits.
You should,
should not.
Not good,
not enough,
not good
enough.

I learned to cultivate
lashes into rows,
tend the open furrows,
braid a circlet of thorns.

Any magician worth
their salt can tell you
that ropes are tightest and cut deepest
when strained against.

The trick is to let go
of breath,
become still,
and let the bindings drop.

Vulnerable

Some paint night soft, the brilliance of fireflies before black.
Others gather gentle sighs, pad the quiet hall of dreams.

Did you know fireflies will eat one another?

A snore ratchets like a broken gear while I toss
the sheets toward another haggard dawn.

Last night a shriek ripped the humid atmosphere,
then a purred hooting drilled talons

into the lunar field of my waking—
there is no mistaking a kill.

Today sunlight swathes every blade of grass,
outlines the garden with a child's crayon.

I watch a bee enter a flower head first,
heedless of danger, or out of options.

We too push into this world, eyes blindly shut.
It pushes back, pushes us to the hard lurid light.

Flying Kites at the Cape

We let the string spool out,
spin and sprint to do our part,
watch teasing fingers
sweep the kite aloft,

shriek for a glorious moment
before the kite dives sharply
to bite the sand, proving
hands cannot control the wind.

I hold the snapshot, culled
from a dusty shoebox
dragged from under the bed.
My father laughs,

his shoulders and hands
hang loose at his sides, while behind
him the dunes of the Cape rise,
domes to the vault of blue above.

It was a rare moment, before
the angry beetled eyes of evening,
before words that swarmed like wasps,
the soured breath of a six pack.

So quickly we grow,
our halcyon days peered at
through faded photos,
with hands that can hold time.

Like Schrodinger's cat we are both
child and old, happy or angry,
and the kite is remembered
as kissing the blue or crashed.

It all depends which lid
we choose to take off the box.

Room of Mirrors

I am five, my eye billows,
a purple bloom.

My mother says *He loves you,*
he just can't love himself.

I think I am something broken
off, like a branch from its tree.

His own father threw glass words.
Gut-eating cancer took him,

left only a picture in a frame.
The next day at school I tell

the teacher I jumped and fell
onto a bedpost. No questions.

A mouth becomes a mirror.
Each mirror wants to replicate.

An arm becomes a wing to cover
the face. I learn to regurgitate.

I am surrounded by mirrors.
His hand carries a cracked

can of sorrows to his mouth,
pours it down the hole.

Role Reversal

She sits on the front steps,
a cut flower in a dry jar,
asking what to do.

My brother has fled the hive,
a twister of angry wasps burned
out with a toke of acrid smoke
and a one-way ticket to boot camp.

My breath tightens, vacuum
behind the glass of a display case,
where wings are pinned to a board.
Words slide into
the smallest locked drawer.

I remember when
she sat next to my bed,
her hand on my back.
Thunderstorm rattling
the window panes
like chattering teeth,
dropping concrete blocks.

I reach down,
touch the bow of her back.

Vernal Pool

Through the cracked window
a lilting soprano of peepers ring
the concert hall of dark, slumber's song.

Dreams, a half-world that drift like mist,
while star glimmer beams to infinity
from the catwalk of the night sky.

Speckled alders lean,
ready to surge spring's stage.
The hoot of an owl percusses my sleep.

A passing shower chops a base groove,
slaps leaves like crumpled programs.
Isn't that just like life, to shake its sticks,

stroke us with unexpected squalls?
Somewhere wind shoves a tree over,
somewhere a taut bowstring snaps.

Dawn steals the show, raises bright notes.
Wispy white chases gray.
Beech bonnet the pool with lime parasols.

I slip the velvet ropes of the house,
glide the cool damp composition, add my own notes.
The vernal pool burgeons with promise.

Spring crescendos, red-backed salamanders
and leopard frogs crawl from tannin-tinged water
as we ready for the next set.

The refrain is familiar, the coda anyone's guess.

The Temple We Carry

The flat-roofed tenement squats,
one in a huddle of vagrants, back
against the wall of the city's east end.

Artifact of the post-war boom,
brick forgets it is just sand and clay,
and the buildings soldier on,

red fists punching the roof of the city.
The kind of place where cats prowl
and yowl after dark, and gunfire cracks

the fragile shell of sleep, a scant mile away.
Still, the grass in the courtyard was green,
the tops of trees lit with gold,

and there were we, just as green, newly wed.
In our boxcar room, spooning in a twin bed,
stoking the fiery joy of hope with our dreams.

After a year we came to a pretty house in a glade,
the expansiveness of fields and woods,
filled it with furniture, then children,

hope's gossamer longings morphed,
seed to flesh, rebar against fault lines
lurking to rupture our perfectly ordered lives.

This temple of the mundane, gilded by the same sun,
in which we bring our same selves,
the same shaker of salt from where we had been.

Waiting Places

Forty weeks and counting,
the tight ball of a peony bud.

A barred owl on a branch listens.

Saturated air, lightning flashes in silence.
Bikers sheltering under a bridge.

Seagulls hovering midday over the beach.

Hollow of an empty mailbox.
Open lattice of a confessional booth.

One deep breath in the sick room, then none.
Freshly dug earth anywhere.

The pause that waits to take us when we are ready.

Morning Sun

After Edward Hopper, Morning Sun

Enters her window
and slaps the wall awake.

She has not slept.

Operating theater green paint
chases afterimages—

a red sunrise hides
behind the wash of blue.

The brick mill's smokestacks
rise like fat cigars.

Red stain in the water
flushes hope down the drain.

White light shines in, frames
the curve of her shoulders,

illumines a corona around her face.
She stares unflinching at the morning sun.

The Year of Bicycles and Geraniums

This world is so often linear,
circumscribed by painted lines
and metal signs. Here,
bicycle wheels swirl,
fibonacci gears turn.
They lean against walls,
clatter across cobblestones
chime bells as they whir past.

A seashell curves
the croissant on my plate,
the cupola of the Duomo di Firenze
parachutes above the piazza.

You pass your hand over
the rounded bump under my ribs,
and I notice how spokes
of your irises reach blue limbal rings,
how the Mediterranean light tips
the curls that brush your collar,
how sun both infuses and reflects,
gives dimension to the whitewashed
stone it touches.

Here are geraniums, leaves lush and scalloped,
all velvet ears and lipsticked mouths.
Impossible cotton candy pinks
and apple reds sing opera in painted boxes,
lean brightly scarfed heads
above wrought iron railings

Joy is a sphere, a bubble that swells
and floats iridescent and ephemeral
from my beating heart.
Too soon, like the new life cartwheeling inside,
to be released on currents beyond control.
A bubble that must float away and burst,
showering tiny droplets wherever it lands.

It is Here, Within, Everywhere

No matter how Eden has tried
to hoard perfection within her walls
it leaps and pours, a high mountain river
cascading from riven clefts.
White froth spills shimmering light,
splits and dives through an evanescent rainbow,
rides backs of chuckling droplets
to the waiting pool.

The stream of love we share surprises me.
My fingers were nimble, learned to play
Flight of the Bumblebee on the flute.
Now my pulse trips in sixteenth notes,
until changing to a slow soft slide
from pinnacle to water lazing below.

We can't keep it to ourselves.
First we were two,
then came a third, a fourth.
Love multiplies, all the while
cracked shells will tumble from a nest.

We may walk on schist, our feet shoeless,
and sun may burn the tips of our ears,
but all the while love
is a small brown apple seed
that swells in our chests.

Sundowning

The India ink of dark descends,
and my mother paces,

swallowed by a shadow
like the antique clock,

cracked and sprung.

A clock overwound is like
a bird with a broken wing,

it cannot tell time, nor can it fly.

I flick on the light switch
and take her hand.

Morning Swim

My brother's thoughts have gaps
like the missing planks of the old pier
since his return.

When the tide is flowing in
he swims in a rockweed garden
teeming with life.

On the ebb, a boneyard of shells shimmer.
His eyes set, thin blade against a relentless sun,
a nystagmus of watchfulness.

Splayed pilings of the pier glisten,
trousered in green velvet, bedecked
with barnacles,

ruined decking slimed and slippery;
dried blood and fish scales
sequin the wood.

Below the pier snapper blues scatter
shiners in an arc. Pelicans patrol,
ever watchful for a mercurial flash.

My brother swims every morning,
the white noise of the surf
erases the detonations he hears,

water wrapping him with amniotic comfort.
The sea shuffles and scourges,
but also brings a hush that surpasses

the burden of endless sorrow,
a buoyancy that lifts the glimmering
light once more to his eyes.

Aftermath

In the full green leaf of July
his spine and rib scaffolded
a semblance of strength,
even as the spool of his thoughts
unraveled, tymbals clicking
over hidden hollows.

A cicada brood molts, leaves
exoskeletons clinging on bark.
He shed his skin by his own hand,
left his husk on last year's leaves.

I too cracked open, shell bit,
soft kernel exposed,
aril of my heart seared.

To burn is to feel, to feel, remember,
but I am tired and sad. I wait
for ashes to scour and purify clouded sight.

When I peel hands from my eyes
will they cup the face of God?

Light and the dissonant drone
of the cicadas fades.

I will not suffer earth to cover me yet.
I still breathe.

In occult blackness I strain
to hear in the hush one hosanna,
even a single set of wings.

I do not think it was easy.

The Profane and Sacred Take Residence in the Same Space

State Police brought the release
for the rifle to be melted, returning
the barrel to a hunk of steel.

A branch snaps, the clock glares 3:05 am.
I shudder, the revenant of death hangs
where the mind turns from trivialities.

I touch my wet cheek, tears right and just
for sufferers in self-imposed solitary, unable
to pick the lock. My thoughts turn back.

My grandmother's tissue-thin, spotted hands,
smoothing a letter from Billy Graham, kept
in the handbag always at her side.

The folded worn dollar bill she would pull
from her vinyl change purse, press into my hand.
She told me she spoke with Jesus in bed.

My mother's hand on my fevered brow,
smoothing rubbing alcohol onto my arms.
Vicks mentholatum rising from my chest.

My newborn nuzzling with rose-bud lips.
Tiny fist grasping one finger,
forehead blemish red from an angel-kiss.

His hand holding mine after the head-on,
boosting me into the pickup, unable
to pull myself up after multiple broken ribs.

My own hands wipe the wet from my cheeks,
wrap around arms and shoulders,
give myself a hug.

Wind, Like Siblings

Sometimes I wake to a white howling,
remembrance tied to a gale of sudden death,
no way to grasp it by the tail.
That tiger keeps its claws sharpened,
never turns to butter.

A gust ripped shingles from his roof.
I learn what I never wanted to know,
how delusions can bloom,
how the mold of darkness
is earless to our concerns.
Dampness finds a way through cracks,
stains creep across ceilings.

I cannot unsee what is locked in my head.
Maybe if I were better schooled
by thrashing treetops, took notice
how the wind batters barn boards,
clacks and chatters window panes—
instead I wrapped myself in hope
an untamed squall would not hone
teeth on me.

But since the storm I have found snickering
mirth from lips of dancing leaves,
surf that smacks a cold wet towel at my legs,
then snatches hats with a big brother of a gust
to skitter and tumble among parking lot flotsam.

Wind. Breathes, shears, rends.
Pushes and pulls waves.
Scatters seeds and detritus alike
to the waiting cradle of earth.
Lifts and drops, whispers
in near stillness when we listen.

Pilgrimage

In a drawer, your hairbrush.
Under the bed, moccasins.
You would slip into them,
supple like a hand sliding
into a jeans pocket,
molding two into one.

My face is stretched,
taut as a drumhead,
just yesterday crumpled,
a paper balled in the trash.
I think of fish heads,
glazed eyes open.

The sight of your cap
on its hook by the door
has corseted my chest.
If only becomes the hinge,
a fulcrum that splits the boning.
I am undone.

A bedlam of jays
sound behind the blinds.
In your closet pressed
shirts hang in a neat row.
There are many rooms
in which to go. I plunge
into the basement.

Would that I could climb
these stairs on my knees
in pilgrimage to the crack
of light above.
Abandon why
as my first thought.
Replace it with don't go.

Sun Glint

Clouds short sheet the sunlight,
I am folded into the crease.
Beneath the bridge still waters
reflect a younger sister, lines etched
from grief's needle, smoothed
by water's sepia tones.

I bend over the railing,
look closer into the water,
tannin-rich from maple and birch.
Leaves that blazed with color
now blackened on the sand.
My leaning blocks the light.

The solstice has visited twice
since I found you lying still.
Days grow shorter while memory
segues to a photograph fading to gray.

I think about the stars,
how they fill the summer night.
How the light in eyes must go somewhere—
I believe it rises
to the last thing seen.

Along the bank a small boy has caught a fish.
You would have cast your line,
eased the hook and slid the fish back
into the water, watched as it wriggled
away, flashing silver. Sometimes
a hook snag is harder to release.

It's often just a pause like this one
in which we collect bits of ourselves
and each other that we imagined lost.
Like clouds that pocket the sun as they pass,
I am still here.

Morning

Sometimes it steals gravity.
The air wears chain mail,
an ostrich foot presses onto my back.

Two-dimensional thoughts thicken,
become ferrous, polycythemia
rafts a turgid river to frontal lobes.

Upon my waking, remnants
of dreams are as useful as an egg-tooth
after the shell falls away,

and tarnished silver needs so much
stroking, best to leave it
dull and in the drawer.

Dreams prick with their kiss,
a Judas sort of friend.
Bird-song saves me, tuned

to dawn's timepiece, each note woven
with murmuring echoes of creation—
and so too am I.

Instinct prompts rising,
and I must shake off
this weight that smothers.

Pin-feathers must be preened,
there are new feathers to grow,
wings to unpinion.
I will fly as best I can.

A Bare Season Past

When the ghost pepper breath of fire exhaled,
immolating the parched undergrowth of summer,
whatever I touched billowed then drifted,
ash to barren ground.

What I carried with me fit into my chest pocket,
tiny as sequoia seeds that sprout only after
they are awakened by searing heat.

December's chill breeze slaps me
into alertness I didn't feel in my warm kitchen.
Ice crusts the snow where I trudge.

When Earth spins it is unfelt,
but when the vat of darkness tips sooner
and the woods grow quiet,
crunch amplifies beneath my boots.

A lone chickadee calls *sweetie* from a spruce.
Animals are scarce, gone to ground,
in torpor that mimics the ice.

The mind sees what it will.
A bent and blackened tree
masquerades as a deer.

A cluster of snow falls
onto my bare neck.
Each flake is a crystalline marvel,

fully formed in its brief flight—
that like us, catches the waning light
for a flicker.

Great Blue Heron at Robert's Pond

In the pooling darkness,
where rushes line the bank,
it stands and stares. I almost miss it,
motionless as a royal guard,
a frippery of feathers on its crown.
Smokey blue greeting dusk,
perched on spindly legs,
with bright amber eyes transfixed
at what lies just below the surface.

How often I have stood and stared,
rooted by indecision, wondering
what I've almost seen
or has just passed by, *there*—
at the very edge of vision.

The heron has no such hesitation.
With a lightning strike
it seizes what it seeks.

A guttural grawnk splits the hush
as the heron points its head,
lifts off and ascends,
then tucks its neck

each slow flap certain and true
into a gray ice sky,
a fletching of legs trailing behind.

Eye of the Sun

Another twenty-four hour spin on the lathe
and I see the miracle of sun above the lake,
twinning with its reflection.

With a crinkle lake twin sends
the chill air a brume of warmth,
while invisible hands juggle the orbs.

Before the first maple leaf
drank the blood of autumn
our brother cheated the encroaching cold.

Humidity swelled, then saturated,
a drowning weight onto bent shoulders
the night he snapped his stem.

Grief is a torn pocket jangling loose change,
hands needed to stitch the hole
appear from surprising places.

I watch the lake blink, the way
a nictitating membrane slides across an eye.
Ice will soon form a shield

and hands that wind the movement
of the sun will stretch apart,
pull back the awning of the sky.

Certain as the spindle that turns
maple on the lathe,
the solstice will arrive.

I will feel the eye of the sun pause
and when the turning begins
I become, burls and all, something new.

Swift Current

These banks once held
a leaning oak

where from long ago
a braided rope was hung—

when we let go
we were the sky.

The water closed
us into its chilled fist,

then popped us like corks
among the bubbles,

to everlasting delight.

We pass by, memory
refreshed by skeletal arms,

the tree reaching up
from its sodden bed,

reverberation of laughter
sounding in our heads.

Lake Cobbosseecontee Reverie

Black water surrounds the pickerelweed,
chuckles faintly as I pass.
Along the path mountain ash lean in with a feathered touch,
and I'm sure I hear leaves snicker
as the breeze tickles by.

On this sunless day the black water hides
its secrets from me,
just as the clouded night swathes itself
in damp wool, then turns its back
on stars that burn in their orbits.

I have learned on such days to skirt the tree roots that reach
to grab my feet, trouble just a step away.
But there are also days when I duck into the shaded chapel
of the hemlocks, and with a glad heart take my rest.

Tomorrow sun will pour out light, wrap leaf and needle
in palest gold, dive into the water
to paint each pebble, and gild the scales of a perch
before it sashays away with a flick of its tail.

I will pick up a stone streaked gorgeously
with gray and pink, colors fading
as it dries in my hand,
and marvel at the alchemy of the moment.

Soon the stone will match those lying
bleached and bland on the beach.
Soon clouds will accumulate to louver shut the window of the sky.
I'll keep walking, past water that is never truly black,
past stones that hold colors of the sunrise.

Rising Tide

Today we dive, full steam ahead
with what can only be joy—
holding breath, lifted by cloud-hands,
our bodies,
ark of whale ribs, sinew of sea otter,
roll to face the sun.

Yesterday we barely dipped a toe,
stayed safely cleat-hitched,
knowing what hides in the deep
can crack us open with one bite.
Yesterday we wore seclusion
like armor plate, convinced of need
to ward off circling sharks.

Rising tides scatter on the shore
spent whelk whorls, quahogs,
the carapace of a horseshoe crab.
How can we swim, let alone tread water
in the face of this casting out?

Storm surges dredge new paths,
estuaries deepen, the tide pours
inexorably into newly carved bowls.
Beyond the white caps water gathers
strength to seethe, smash, foam.

We can't always explain what
scrapes and lays bare our resistance.
We grow fatigued of caution, tired
of our dun-colored selves, ready to don
iridescence, even for a moment.

The clamorous tide exhales
and we rush as it tongues the shore,
to taste and eat everything,
moon crazed, until the final ebb.

Nancy Sobanik has poems curated by *Hole In The Head Review, Eclectica, MacQueen's Quinterly, Synkroniciti, One Art, Triggerfish Critical Review, Anti-Heroin Chic, Sparks of Calliope, Sheila-Na-Gig, The Ekphrastic Review, Verse-Virtual*, and various anthologies.

She was an editorial assistant for Alice James Books, screening manuscripts for The 2025 Alice James Award. An active member of the Maine Poet's Society, she also participates in the poetry community through the Maine Writers and Publishers Alliance. She has studied poetry through workshops led by notable Maine poets Betsy Sholl (Poet Laureate 2006–2011), Cate Marvin, Arisa White, Julia Bouwsma (Poet Laureate (2021- 2026), Stuart Kestenbaum (Poet Laureate 2016–2021) and Sarah V. Schweig.

A finalist in the 2025 Maine Chapbook Series, she has won awards in the Maine Postmark Poetry Contest judged by Tim Seibles, Dianelly Antigua and Kirun Kapur; the Eastport Arts Center Charles Moore Poetry Prize Competition and The Poet's Corner Art and Ekphrastic Poetry Contests.

Special thanks is extended to Timothy Green, Editor, for the mfa workshop experience of *Rattle*'s Critique of the Week, Poets Respond and Rattlecast, programs which have been instrumental in developing poetic craft.

Social Media Tags:
https://nancysobanik.substack.com/
https://www.facebook.com/nancy.sobanik/
nancysobanik.bsky.social

www.ingramcontent.com/pod-product-compliance
Lightning Source LLC
LaVergne TN
LVHW090541110826
845146LV00003B/1219
9798899904806